Journeys

Journeys

*A Collection of Poems
About Life, Love, Faith
and Determination*

Marcia Ranglin-Vassell

JOURNEYS
A COLLECTION OF POEMS ABOUT LIFE, LOVE, FAITH AND DETERMINATION

iUniverse books may be ordered through booksellers or by contacting:

iUniverse
1663 Liberty Drive
Bloomington, IN 47403
www.iuniverse.com
1-800-Authors (1-800-288-4677)

Because of the dynamic nature of the Internet, any web addresses or links contained in this book may have changed since publication and may no longer be valid. The views expressed in this work are solely those of the author and do not necessarily reflect the views of the publisher, and the publisher hereby disclaims any responsibility for them.

Any people depicted in stock imagery provided by Getty Images are models, and such images are being used for illustrative purposes only. Certain stock imagery © Getty Images.

ISBN: 978-1-5320-7231-4 (sc)
ISBN: 978-1-5320-7232-1 (e)

Print information available on the last page.

iUniverse rev. date: 07/12/2019

Contents

Chapter One
LOVE LOST ... LOVE GAINED

Chapter Two

THE STRUGGLE IS REAL...THE FIGHT CONTINUES

Chapter Three

NOT SO RANDOM POEMS

Foreword

I didn't find poetry, poetry found me. My poems are inspired by love, family, violence, faith, nature-everything. As a teen, I tried hard to make sense of the nonsense that was woven into my everyday life. Poetry rescued me. I would hide under the almond tree in our yard and write about my hopes, fears, and aspirations. I would write about the love that I wanted, and the love that was so beautiful yet so elusive. I wasn't sure if I even knew what love was, but thinking about it was beautiful as well as magical.

I wrote my first poem *Who is God?* when I was fourteen years old. It was an entry in our church's national poetry competition. I didn't know I would win. I didn't even think about winning. I simply wanted to express my innermost feelings about my new found Faith in God. In addition, there was political unrest and violence in my neighborhood so in writing this poem, I tried to reconcile my Faith in a loving God with the turmoil and conflict around me.

I remember not being able to attend the competition because I didn't have anything to wear that was new enough or looked good enough for a competition at church headquarters in Kingston. I got the news of my winning the day after the competition from Pastor Davis, the fiery minister at our church. I remember submitting the poem but hadn't thought much about it after. Needless to say, winning was a huge surprise.

I've always loved poetry. I love reciting poems, and I enjoy listening to others reading poetry. I remember as a fifth grade student having to recite poems such as *Daffodils* by William Wordsworth or *The Creation* by James Weldon Johnson. I enjoy Louise Bennett's Dialects. They are raw and written in Jamaican patois. When I was fifteen years old I was selected to participate in a "tryout" for a national competition at the YWCA. The poem I chose to recite was ***Dutty Tough*** by Louise Bennet. I remember getting stage fright right after saying the title of the poem. It could have been the large crowd in the audience. I'm not sure but I could not remember one word of the poem after I said the title. I was mortified. I don't remember if I cried or what happened during the moments of me not remembering my lines and me leaving the stage. It's still a fog.

I've written hundreds of poems over the years. Growing up in our small close knit community most of my friends enjoyed my poetry. My poems didn't just belong to me; they belonged to my community. I would lend poems to any and everyone who wanted to show off their oratory skills at local concerts or at competitions. I cherished the moments when I had an audience of teenagers around the "Housing Scheme" where we lived listening to my poems. "Scheme" as everyone called it had 26 two room board houses for families. Our family lived at Lot number twenty-three Cambridge Farm Housing Scheme. Decades later, I'm still trying to figure out how dad made room in our two room house for total strangers.

I wish I knew how meaningful my poems were back then. The first time I realize the impact they had on others was when I went home in 2016. Norman, whom everyone called Sikey, asked me to recite ***Mr Big Man.*** Before I had the chance to begin, he belted out the words **"Oppression, Starvation Victimization Seems Their Theme."** My heart smiled.

My poems are usually about real people and real events but mostly about love. I am not a complex woman, and my poems are not complex either. I see the world and its problems from compassionate human lens. I mourn for the poems that I have lost. I hope that somewhere in the universe my words are bringing hope to someone who needs them.

In writing this collection, I dug into my memory bank and rummaged through old journals and notebooks. The poems represent different stages of my life. Of course, I am still evolving but for now, I am this totally flawed human being owning my space in the universe while trying to make a difference in the lives of others. It is my hope that **Journeys** will perch upon the tablet of someone's heart and guide him or her to a place of peace or a Call to Action.

Dedication

I dedicate this collection of poems in the loving memory of my father, Eric Ranglin who continues to inspire me every day and to my mom, Mavis Ranglin for her strength and tenacious spirit. In spite of all the troubles that mom went through or those that my siblings and I put her through, she remains solid as a rock. Mom lost dad when she was fifty-four years old. I can't imagine how she got through it but she did. Dad was a larger-than-life man, not very tall in stature but big on dreams and with a heart of gold. My dad was such a visionary, and I appreciate the legacy that he left behind.

Mom is my Shero, she stands by me in the most difficult of situations. She is one of the most important anchors in my life. She was senior advisor to the two primary campaigns that I ran. Mom had a near fatal fall in 2017. After spending over a month in rehabilitation, she came home. It was a rough road to recovery, but because of her determination, drive and courage, she is back to living an independent life. Thank you Mom for teaching me the true meaning of perseverance.

About The Book

*J*ourneys is a collection of poems written between 1974 and 2019. The poems are personal in nature and takes readers on an interesting journey through time. *Journeys* represent the past, the present, and the future. This anthology is intended to captivate its readers by taking them on a journey that begins in the ghettos of Bull Bay and ends up (for now) miles away in Providence, Rhode Island.

Journeys will captivate its readers by bringing the richness of one woman's desire to escape the ravages of poverty. *Journeys* delve deeply into love, hope, resilience, and everything in between. It has a rich Caribbean flavor that lures readers to the exotic "paradise" island of Jamaica with white sand beaches as well as to its zinc fences and "concrete jungles."

Journeys shed light on issues of race, gender, colorism and class among other social constructs. The poems peek into one woman's experience and her constant struggle to use her voice, and to be heard amidst the "noise." Each poem is sure to either soothe readers' soul or prick their social conscience to activism for justice.

Journeys will not disappoint readers. The poems are happy, sad, lonely, and hopeful. They draw from the poet's lived experiences as a young girl growing up on the island to that of a mother, wife, sister, auntie, friend, teacher and legislator. *Journeys* will inspire readers everywhere. It will provide support, affirmation, guidance, consolation and laughter. *Journeys* is a work of the heart, and a timeless treasure that everyone should have in their collection.

About The Author

Marcia Ranglin-Vassell's improbable journey took her from her hometown in Bull Bay, Jamaica to the Rhode Island General Assembly. She grew up in poverty. Like so many children from similar background, she did not have many materials things. "I still remember everything that I owned; I remember every dress, shoes, book bag-everything." "The fact that I hardly had any material things of value made me realize quite early in life that "stuff" could not define me but rather my words and my character".

Her world views are influenced by the value system that her parents inculcated in their nine children. Marcia believes "You work hard, you respect people, you believe in the power of God to do wonderful things, and you give to your community your talents, your treasures and your time."

Books gave Marcia wings. She remembers curling up in bed with a book just to escape the harsh realities around her. Nowadays, she does the same for children. One of her greatest achievements is going back to her old neighborhood to donate fiction and nonfiction books as well as school supplies to kids in need. Marcia also has an annual holiday drive where she collects books and school supplies for children in her local House District. It is her hope that the donated books are providing wings to the children.

Marcia holds a Diploma in Elementary Education from Saint Joseph's Teachers' College in Kingston, Jamaica, a Bachelor's degree in Community Health Education from Rhode Island College, a Grades 7-12 Certification in English and a Masters of Arts degree in Special Education from Providence College.

Marcia is a public servant who cares deeply about her family and her community. She has a passion for service and abhors injustice. She was recipient of the Dr. Rose Butler Browne Award from Rhode Island College in 1994 for working with disadvantaged populations. In 2007, she received the Women of Achievement Award from the YWCA, Northern, Rhode Island. She received the 2011 Community Health Education Service Award from Rhode Island College. Marcia was the recipient of the 2016 Excellence in Education Award from her Alma Mater, Yallahs High School. In 2016, Marcia was named "10 to Watch" by Providence Monthly. She earned the 2018 Community Leadership Award from the Jamaica Association of Rhode Island for her work with the Diaspora. She received the Powerful, Independent, Notoriously, Knowledgeable (P.I.N.K) Award from a multicultural women's group at the University of Rhode Island. She also received the Excellent Leadership Award from African Heritage Women in Education and Empowerment (AHWEE) in recognition for her outstanding leadership, noteworthy achievements, and contributions towards the progress of children, women and families. Marcia's name is synonymous with excellence. She has received numerous other recognitions and citations for her commitment and work towards to justice. She uses her voice to elevate the issues of education, race, gender, poverty, inequality, and gun violence.

Representative Ranglin-Vassell lives in Providence, Rhode Island with her husband Van Vassell and her sons Van Jr., and twin sons Eric and Terrence. Her daughter Alethe lives in Atlanta, GA. She has two handsome grandsons, Joseph and Elias; they are her pride and joy. Marcia is a born again Christian. She teaches high school in the city of Providence. She believe that education is a basic human right. Marcia is currently a member of the Rhode Island General Assembly. She is a Progressive Democrat who was first elected in 2016. Her motto is "I have no obstacles in my life, I turn all of them into stepping stones." Her favorite scripture is Jeremiah 29:11. She is a member of Ebenezer Baptist Church in Providence, Rhode Island.

Acknowledgements

My thanks first, and foremost to God, who guides my path and strengthens me every day. Much love and gratitude to my dearest husband, Van Vassell, for catching me before I fall, and to my children, Alethe, Van Jr., Eric and Terrence. My life would be ridiculously boring without you guys, so thank you! Thank you to my two beautiful grandsons Joseph and Elias who make me smile all the time! Being a grandmother is such a beautiful gift from God.

Thank you to my sisters, Pearline, Valrie and Lisa who are my absolute best friends! I get to talk to you for hours on end. I love being able to be totally unfiltered with you, and for that I am forever grateful. To my brothers Lloyd, Burchell, Basil, Donovan and Desmond – thank you all for taking care of me and having my back. We are, and will remain "The Ranglin Posse." Thank you to my nieces and nephews especially my nephews Fidel who was "my first son" as well as my amazing godson Rexroy. To my cousin Olive and my "first daughter" Donna who I got to "experiment" being a mom with at twelve or thirteen years old. To all of my in-laws, thank you for being there for me.

To my primary school and church friends, Marcia, and Bridgette, my high school friends especially Cynthia, my college friends especially Jean and Lurline. To my "new" friends Michael, Kathy (Kate), Ursula, Andy, Jill, and Lisa. To my campaign managers Grizzel and Kadeem, thank you for helping me to win not one but two hard fought primary elections.

Thank you to my teachers at Bull Bay All Age School, especially Paula Edwards who made sure that I got free "extra lessons" (tutoring) when mom and dad had no money to pay for those lessons. Back then, kids had to pay for "extra lessons" as we prepared to take those "dreadful" examinations which were prepared in England. Those exams might have set the stage for me not being a fan of standardized tests, who knows.

Thank you to my dad who could not read or write but who was wise enough to start a basic school (pre-school) and a church in 1963. The church-school was pretty simple. It was under a tarpaulin in our front yard. My little friends and I would sit on wood planks held up by cinder blocks as we learned our *A, B, Cs, I, 2, 3s*. Thanks to Sister Fisher, the deaconess in our church who taught me how to read. By the time I was 6 years old and got to Primary School I was already reading. Today, the Eleven Miles New Testament Church of God and Windsor Basic School still operates because of the vision my dad had so many moons ago.

My love and gratitude to the Eleven Miles community that cradled me amidst the poverty, and gun violence. To my friends who are also my cousins – Maxine, Linda, Marry (whose real name is Maria), and Nelly (whose real name is Anzonetta), thank you for the ring games we played- *Dandy Shandy, Brown Girl In The Ring, What Can you Do, London Bridge* and so many other games that would entertain us for hours. I'm sure the games took our minds off the harsh realities of our lives.

To all the little old ladies (who are no longer here) Ms. Rhoda who would send me to "shop" and let me keep the change, Ms. Blanche, Ms. Ethel and Aunt Lou who was not my real aunt but whom I called Aunt Lou anyway. I got to hear all the gossip in the world because they were my grandmother's best friends. Thanks to my grandmother Lillian "Gady" Mignott who was a no nonsense woman with a "light hand". Gady trusted me to write her letters but would not spare the rod if she thought I was too chatty or fresh. Thank you to my friend Trevor (whose real name is Anthony) and whose friendship I'll always cherish, and to his mother, Lillian "Ms. Lill" Walker (no longer here with us) who helped to make my college experience at St. Joseph's a bit easier. To my extended family, friends, and supporters who are too numerous to name individually, thank you for your love and support. Finally, thank you to the Universe as she continues to provide me with positive energy to continue my life's mission-***Fighting For All of Us.***

Marcia

If you're reading this then I assume that you know my aunt, Marcia Ranglin-Vassell, so to you this script might be redundant. However, if you do not know of Marcia then please allow my words to introduce you. She is kind, hardworking and resilient in her beliefs. She is a fighter, always there in your corner when you need her. Most of all, Marcia is one of the most selfless people that I know. She is wife, mother, sister, friend and aunt, but most of all she is phenomenal.

Of her many qualities, what stands out most is her hard-work ethics and her strength. She is never one to shy away from challenge, always on the run, and never stopping to take time for herself. It's actually very foolish to me, but to her it is a necessity. Giving up never crosses her mind because she is aware that what she does today impacts tomorrow. It's the quality in her that I admire the most.

I recall her being the first mother I can remember. Back when I lived in Jamaica, it was Marcia who would make sure I was ready for school and made sure I ate at night. I remember in 1988 there was a hurricane and she put me in a cardboard box. Keeping an eye on me, she made sure I was fine without obvious worry for her own safety. That's my Auntie Mar.

Marcia Ranglin- Vassell is a teacher. Not only is teaching her profession but it's something she does all of the time. On the surface it gets boring, but when you walk away her words are always on your mind. I can easily state that is what makes Marcia great. Nobody would disagree. But such usage of a word so weak and only one syllable would be an injustice to her.

So in closing I say, when you see her, when you hear her, when you touch her... Remember not that she is: wife, mother, sister, aunt, friend... but remember simply that you are in the presence of a phenomenal woman.

B.A. Ranglin

B.A. Ranglin is my nephew, I was his sole guardian from 1984-1988. He wrote this tribute in 2010.

Chapter One

To Be Like Mama

You are everything
That I want to be
Mama.

You have given up so much
Your hopes, your dreams
Your aspirations
Your life.

It seems so senseless
That you have made
Such sacrifice
In the name of love.

I've seen you struggle, Mama
It wasn't easy
After Dada went home to be with God
But, you stayed strong
And, you held on
When many would have given in
Or, given up.

I've seen you cried
Only once mama
And, that's because you cried
At the loss
Of a family member.

You are at your strongest
Whenever
The going gets tough
Determination is in your veins.

"If I have to wear leaves"
You once said
"My children must be educated."
You are distinguished
My fair one
Ninety
And, still going strong.

I watch you
Grudgingly
Standing at the kitchen counter
Making dumplings, peas soup
Porridge
Rice an' peas an' chicken
Oxtail and Callaloo
Carrot Juice
Potato pudding.

How many times
Have I told you
"Mom, you don't have to."
You will not stop
You feel compelled
To love.

I love you, Mama
You are the heart and soul
Of this family
My family
Our family
So wise

Your wisdom
Infinite.

May you continue to live
Your hopes, your dreams
Your aspirations
Through generations
That will follow.

To be like Mama
My hopes
My dreams
My aspirations
To be like Mama
So beautiful
So wise
So strong.

Stay With Me

For all the times you have loved me
stood up for me
cradled me
you are my strength
And, I would be nothing without you.

Stay with me my love
we are so much better
together
"How can I say thanks to you,
my love?"
I really can't
Your love is boundless.

I look adoringly into your eyes
and, see an incredible reservoir of compassion
for those still living
on the so-called fringes of society
I can never measure up to you, my love
my ineptitude of loving another human being the way you love me
your willingness to love
While expecting nothing in return is above me.

Stay with me, my love
let's make new memories, together
walking along white sand beaches
sand tickling between our toes

eating vine ripe mangoes
Juice dripping down our arms and caressing our fingers.

I love you so much
my limited lexicon cannot express how much you mean to me
you are my sun, my moon, my stars
my world!
just stay with me and be my love.
And, I will love you for a lifetime.

I wrote this poem as mom recuperated from an almost tragic fall in 2017.

Love Prose For My Grandmother

I threw my arms around her
We, in tender embrace
Her small but strong frame caressed me gently
She whispered silently in my ears
"I never thought I would ever see you again."
"You are my flesh and blood," she whispered.

I held her close to me
Tightly
I fell in love with her, all over again
I wept
For only once before had I felt her body so close to mine
Now, I could feel the bond of love that neither time nor place could ever erase
Tears filled my eyes,
And joy my heart
She cuddled like a babe in my arms
"How could I have let this precious one out of my life for so long?"

I sobbed, unable to control myself
Her eyes glowed as she rocked me to and fro like a babe in her arms
She begins to sing
What melody to my ears
I stopped to think where I had heard such beautiful singing
It came back to me
Dad had the same sweet melodious voice
My soul rejoiced in the thought
She looked me dead in the eyes and recited some prose
Prose, that only she could compose.

I am captivated by her beauty, her radiance, memory and strength
Her smile illuminates the room in which we were sitting
I clung to her small frail body
Not wanting to let go
We cried together
Knowing that this was not going to last much longer
I whispered in her ears "I love you Grandma and Dada loves you too."
With tears in her eyes she whispered,
"I love you too."
We embraced one last time
Kissed each other passionately
And then said, "goodbye."

I wrote this poem to eulogize my grandmother, Ellen Spencer (1893-2006).

Autumn

Chirping birds
solemnly packed multi-colored leaves
piercing cold temperatures on my brown face
tranquil, but fierce wind
Me, enveloped by this beautiful fall morn
My soul rejoices at the thought
that I, a child of the universe
can find peace and gratitude
In this often complex world.

Joggers, enjoying the morning run
minding their own business
as well they should
perhaps, distant from the magnitude of
what lies ahead
that makes so much sense though
maybe, maybe... not
weaving in and out of traffic
swift feet
Safely to the other side.

Me, wrapped tightly in my thoughts
trying to make sense of the incomprehensible
a thousand answers flood my mind
"Where are the questions?"
Hail?
"Where did this beautiful shower come from?"
I stand here, in total awe and gratitude at the awesome nature of my God!

and with a keen realization that
Love is so much stronger than hate
It is that love that propels me to this sacred place
in Mama's kitchen around the table where peace rescues me
From the harsh realities of life.

Inhaling the exotic smell of oxtail seasoned with that Walker's Wood Jerk
Sauce
Gungo peas, simmering in coconut milk on the stove
Mom moving at her own pace
and, with romantic precision and grace
making decisions about Thanksgiving
"Yuh okay Mar?"
Mom in her beautiful Jamaican patois
"Yes, Mom mi good."
Our conversation wanders off
Mom stirs her oxtail
defying Jen's order that she doesn't have to make anything
but, that's my mom
She control her universe by doing what she knows and feels is right
maybe, I'll take Luna out for a walk
Maybe, because it's still beautifully cold outside.

Luna is my son's beautiful 65 pounds Pitbull rescue dog. On tough days, I like to curl up in bed with her. She's such a therapy dog.

Still No Answers

We have no pictures of you, dad
We can never show our children what you look like
We have no audio of you, dad
We can never have our children listen to the songs you sung, or the stories
you told
But,
What we have is your legacy, dad
The life you lived, the love you shared.

Sometimes I think it strange that we have no pictures of you, dad
To look lovingly in your eyes, to smile with you, to laugh with you
But, what we have is all of us
Yes, all of us
The nine of us
The only physical evidence of you that you left mom
And, by extension that you left all of us.

Every single one of us have a part of you, dad
The walk, the smile, the voice, the legacy, the soul
We can't fill your shoes, dad
So, we will not even try
They are just too big, and our feet too small
But, we will try to do as you did, dad
To love as you loved
To care as you cared.

Your words will always linger lovingly in our hearts, dad
"I am here to feed the poor and needy."

"How could you when you yourself was in need at times?"
Your lesson of giving has taught us that you don't need much to give more
"I have never met a stranger", you always said
"How could that be, dad?"
Simple, everyone you met was your friend.

You never learned how to read or write, dad
But, you built a church-school in the front of our yard
I'm sure you know that the church-school still goes on, dad
Giving thousands of little children the education you yourself could only dream of
So, on this Father's Day, dad
Another Father's Day without even a picture of you
I just want to say, how I miss and love you
Thank you for the memories
Your legacy lives on in the nine of us
And, in the generations that follow
Thank you for leaving us with a Compass for daily living, dad
Forever with the Angels, but gone, way too soon.

Love Poem For My Sister

Life ain't easy, Val
Juggling a thousand and one balls
Deciding which to let fall
Knowing which ones to hold on to
Life ain't easy, Val
When things are falling all over the place
When you're stuck
And, you don't know how to move
In those moments
When all you see is despair
It's comforting to know
You have a shoulder to lean on
Someone to dry your tears
Someone who believes
In you
Totally
Unconditionally.

My sister, my friend…my love
Infinite, unpredictable
Beautiful as Dick Sea
On those long hot dreary days
Bountiful as spring time
In Button Bay.

You will forever be my Shero, Val
The smart one
The take charge one

The beautiful one
The one that makes the most
Complex problem…disappear
The one that life seem so grossly unfair to
But, you remain strong
Always looking out for me
Even in those times that I'm undeserving of your love
And your attention.

I'll always look up to you, Val
My sweet rose
My strong Cactus
Adorned with the beautiful flowers
You're my Lignum Vitae
Strong, powerful…unassuming
I've always wanted to be just like you, Val
But, never quite able to measure up
To your brilliance.
It seem senseless to even try
You're a natural
Not man made.

How can I say thank you, Val
When I don't have the right words
To display my gratitude
For all the times
You've stood up for me
Protected me
Fought for me
Calmed my fears
Dried my tears.
For those times
When you made sure
I had my tuna sandwich for lunch
When I didn't care to bring a sandwich of my own.

You've never let me down, Val
Knocking on doors
In the broiling sun
Sure it was no fun
As you took a tumble
You never complained
Although visibly in pain.
You had a plan
You knew I would be the one
And, yes
You believed in me!

Life ain't easy, Val
For you
For me
For us
We are sisters, and will always be
Strong, beautiful, resilient
You are my Rock of Gibraltar
My bridge over troubled waters
You make sexy looks easy
Your grace
Your beauty
Your strength
You.

I love you, Val
You never flew away from the ghetto
even when you had wings
You stayed with us
All of us
How unselfish can one be
Always putting others first
Giving, yet expecting nothing in return.
Maybe,
Just maybe

One day
I'll be able to measure up
To you, Val
And, if we have time
Let's… plant flowers.

Tonight

Tonight, I write this poem for you
You're the light of my life
Shelter from the storm
Rainbow on those long dreary days
The day I met you
Changed the trajectory of a sad and lonely life
I am so delighted I am your wife.

Tonight, I write this poem for you
Your strength, incomparable
Life has been unkind to you
But you have never wallowed in self pity
Never been resentful
Never allowed yourself to become blue
You always look on the bright side
The beautiful side, the kind side… of life.

Tonight, I write this poem for you
You are all I ever wanted
I am in constant bliss
My heart's filled with gratitude
The universe has brought these two hearts together
May they remain, inseparable
In death, do us part.

Tonight, I write this poem for you
For you, for you, for you
Tonight, I write this poem for you.

Faith

For all the times
That you have put up with me
Cared for me
For those times when life has dealt you a horrible blow
For all the times that you remained strong
When I wanted to give up
You remained relentless
You're an amazing man
Such a treasure
To have, to hold, to love
Please know that my heart belongs to you
Forever!

Without You

I glimpse into your eyes
And, is reminded of a love
That will last a lifetime
You are my fresh vase of roses
Butterflies dancing in the rain
Jolly ranchers on long boring days
You wipe every tear from my eyes
Put a pep in my step
I know we have been through so much together
And, for that… our love must last forever!

Love Poem For My Sons

If only I could
wrap you in my bosom
and, shield you from harm
If only I could be like a cocoon
protecting the soon to be butterfly
I love you more than
you could ever conceptualize
much more than you will
ever realize.
I can't help thinking
how harsh this world is to your kind
docile, meek and mild
You have wings, sons
And, so you must fly
Spread your wings my sweet doves
Jehovah is always watching from above
And as always
keep God
At the center of all you do
And everything will be just fine.

Gentle Breeze

Sitting in the shade with you, my Love
Two hearts beating as one
Still trying to fathom where you've been so long
Feel the gentle breeze caress our bodies
Palm trees dancing to music that only the two of us can hear
Birds chirping, signifying that love will always find a way.

Sitting in the shade with you, my love
Reminiscing about all the good times we've had
Moments that are etched in our hearts forever
Soul mate now, and soulmate forever
Love is complicated, yes, it is
But, I am so glad you found me
And, I'll be sure to never let you go
Sitting in the shade with you, my Love...

Morning Dew

I woke up this morning
And you're not here
But your spirit still lingers in my soul
You are my special gift
And, that is why I'm
Missing you so much.

I love you so much
When you're with me
I soon realize just how much
I miss you when you're away
My hopes and dreams for you are palpable.
I want only the best for you, my love
Go ahead, beyond the sky is your limit
You're young, bold, articulate, and wise
One thing I ask of you, my Love
Is that you keep God at the center of all you do
And, everything will be just fine.

Elias

My sweet little brown face boy
Deep roasted
Chocolate
Eyes brightly shine
Illuminating my path
My guiding light to the goodness in all of humanity
You bring me joy
Your chuckles, your smile eases the pain
If it's even for a while
Your eyes follow me around the room
Like a shepherd keeping watch o'er her flock
Protecting them from harm
It seems so strange
Considering truth be told
You're only a few months old.

You came in my life
at the opportune time
Giving me hope that
All will be fine
Things are a bit topsy turvy right now
I'm trying to make sense
Of this madness
Sadness, babies crying for their mommies
Caravans of the weak
Blisters on their feet
Fleeing violence, poverty

Hoping that one day Lady Liberty
Will hold them in tender embrace.

My sweet little brown face boy
May you continue to bring me Joy!

I fell July 4ᵗʰ and fractured my spine. My grandson Elias was born July 23ʳᵈ 2018.

Weary Wanderer

Love will find its way
Through snow drift mountains
Oceans, land or sea
On those long stormy nights
When the ground's frozen with snow
When all you hear is the howling wind
Whistling to signal a long lost love
When the tulips are trying their hardest to peep
Old man winter is unforgiving and doesn't care a damm.
Come rest upon my boson
Weary, worn wanderer
You might have lost your way
The light house covered in snow
While your dainty feet to the merciless wind sway
There's no refuge in sight
Love endures such awful plight
Your teardrop falls upon a rose bud
And, it illuminates your path
Through deep, thick, unsightly mud
Silently hoping and praying that
Someday...Love... will find its way.

Chapter Two

Mr. Big Man

Oppression, Starvation, Victimization
Seems their theme
"Why can't they see what I have seen?"
Don't oppress me
Mr. Big man
Remember, we are one
Not because you drive a big car
But, if you oppress me, you are for war.
Don't starve me
Mr. Big man
Remember, you are the one
The one I use to carve wood for to make you strong
If you do that, then you're wrong.
Don't victimize me
Mr. Big man
Remember, we're all civilized ones
Not because you're rich, and I am poor, white and I am black
But, because we're one under God's rock
Oppression, Starvation, Victimization
Seems their theme
Why, can't they see what I have seen?

I wrote this poem in 1976 in response to inflation and large scale war on the poor and on the working class.

Repatriation

I was dragged, whipped and brought out
Out of my homeland, Africa
My back was chained to a wall, and all I could do was holler and bawl
I bawl
Whoa, whoa, whoa
When will I be free?
When will I get liberty?
When will I be repatriated back, back to my homeland Africa?

_____

I wrote this poem c. 1975

Small Boy

Wrap Hope in your bosom
and, never let it go
'cause when Hope is gone
life is like an empty Piñata
only meant to disguise
See, the small boy
skipping along Academy Avenue
All of six or seven years old
big back-pack clings to his small tender frame
Hope, wraps him like a warm blanket
Protecting him from harm
All he can do is hope
hope, that someday he will become a man.

A young man
Twenty-three or thereabout
watches tenderly
As this young lad hops on to the yellow school bus
Now, alone with his thoughts
Thinking of systems that have failed him
turned on him, belittled him… emasculated him

Yet, this young man clutches to Hope
If, only that which lies deep in the soul of the small boy
with the big back- pack.

Wrap, Hope in your bosom
And, never let it go

hope- that someday this
Small boy with the big back- pack
Filled with dreams
will one day become the head of his school
the scientist who will find a cure for cancer
or the President that will one day make Hope and Change a reality
Wrap Hope in your bosom
And, never let it go.

I Thoughht I Could Write A Poem

I thought, I could write a poem
until I realized, I could not, write a poem
So much on my mind
so much to fight for
living wages
kids in cages
How sad.
Makes me mad.
Livid.

I thought, I could write a poem
until I realized, I could not, write a poem
My body
filled with pain
a constant reminder
of my fight for justice
Our fight, for justice.

I thought, I could write a poem
about Hope, hope that someday
We can lay down and rest
Rest from a labor
that's been forced upon us
Forced upon us by a system of oppression and humiliation
Dragged, whipped, chained
stripped of our identity
Or, so they think.

"Get up
stand up
stand up for your right."
Bob ain't here, but his words still lingers in my ears
I have no fear
Redemption is near
We must continue
the good fight of faith
we're on the right side of... Herstory.

Justice should not be blind
this fight, is for all humankind
Black, white, yellow
Brown skinned
the voiceless
the too afraid to speak
the weak
the guy in the barbershop
listening to
Kendrick Lamar's
"How Much A Dollar Cost"
The mom who sits up
all night waiting
for her boy to open the door...
so she can fall asleep.

I thought, I could write a poem
until I realized
Alas! I can write a poem
I can write a poem about, Hope
hope, that one day
We'll be judged not by the color of our skin, religion, wealth
or the lack thereof
but by our character
By the way
we treat those

considered not good enough
not smart enough
not worthy… Enough.

I thought, I could write a poem

A poem… a poem… a poem…
I thought I could write a… poem.

This poem was written in response, and as a reaction to Trump's horrific immigration policies

Some Woman From Jamaica

When you see me
When you hear me
When you support me
When you pray…for me
When you love me, know that
I'm "Some Woman from Jamaica."
Those words weren't meant to celebrate me
Elevate me
They were meant to
Knock me
Dismiss me
Degrade me
Insult… me
Render me… nameless
Yet…they empowered me.

My campaign was never about me
It was about young men
Black men… Brown… men
Getting shot and killed
Their blood soaked in the ground
I ain't your typical politician
Not, even close
I'm by the People for the People
Power… to the People
A product of the ghetto

Fighting… for all of us
Fighting… and never giving up.

My improbable journey takes me from the ghettos of Jamaica
From the small little town of Eleven Miles along The Bay
To the halls of the Rhode Island State House
I'm a Disrupter
Disrupting the Status Quo
I sit in the front row
Seat number 12
Jesus had 12 disciples, that's an idea
"Why am I even here?"
Feeling like a square peg in a round hole
All this rhetoric, makes me mad. Sad.
"Can we just focus on changing real people's lives?"
"Why is this so much about Fat Cats and Corporations?"
"And, what about …Reparations?"
You came to drink milk, not count cows
You were born to stand out not fit in so don't even try.
For now, continue to fight… your redemption is in sight.
Resist.

A Poem For Every Black Woman

Nanny of the Maroons is to Jamaicans what Harriet Tubman is to African Americans
I'm no Nanny of the Maroons or Harriet Tubman
Not even close
I'm simply a Black Woman
Owning my space in a world filled with racism, sexism, bigotry and misogyny
Co-existing in a space where there is war to silence the voice of the Black Woman.

One of these days
You'll hear my story
Her story
Our story
All of it
From Genesis to Revelation
From A to Z
We will shout it from the mountain top
The hope, courage, determination that's laced in our veins
One of these days
You'll hear my story, her story
Our story
Of fighting back
Of never giving up or giving in.

Our lives have not been easy
traversing the Atlantic
O'er oceans, lands and seas

Cotton gins
Sugar cane mills
The oppressors tried and failed
They will never be able to take our dignity
Lands yes, resources yes
But, they can never break the spirit of the Black Woman
The Ashanti Woman. The Asante Woman.

In chains we fought back
channeling the authentic power of Women Warriors
Like Yaa Asanteewaa, like Lillian Mignott, like Ellen Euphema Spencer
And, yes like my personal Shero, Mavis, the Ranglin Warrior
Today, we call on the powers of Nanny of the Maroons, Harriet Tubman
And, every Black Woman who have lived, fought, and died.
There's no retreat for us
Our lives depend on it
Our children's lives depend on it
We know how to fight
We know how to win
Our ancestors have done it
We are doing it
We are, the indomitable Black Woman
Black Woman… Black Woman… Black Woman…

This poem is written in response to the deliberate effort by the Status Quo and those in "power" to silence the voices of Black Women. They are afraid of the truth, and so they find different ways and different means to try to silence our voices. In every instance, they have failed.

America O' America

I wanted to write a springtime poem
Tulips popping out their heads
Daffodils
April showers bring May flowers
I wanted to write a springtime poem
giddy high school seniors
with six weeks to go
I wanted to write a poem about Love.

Yet, I find myself writing
a sad poem
an angry poem
a poem that makes we wonder why
"Why can't all of us be treated with the same level of human dignity?"

Fingers crossed, maybe…maybe one day
I won't have to write a sad poem
about black men being slaughtered like hogs
their blood soaked in the ground
mothers crying
"We want justice."
children denied the opportunity
to see or even know their fathers
Locked away… unjustly.

Today I write a poem
about black boys… gunned down
Before they become men

Bullets flying
intended target
Unarmed… black men. Lying in the streets
Their lifeless body
Surrounded by the speechless throng
Another one…gone too soon.

You're taking our boys
You're taking our men
three strikes and you're out
the so called war on drugs
Crack cocaine, Ganga, weed, marijuana, cannabis whatever you want to
call it
prison cells
Black men
Shackled and penned.

"Bring me your tired."
"Bring me your weary."
"Bring me your poor."
Help us Lady Liberty
We are simply immigrants
seeking the American Dream
Yes, that illusive American Dream.

I wanted to write a springtime poem
Tulips popping out their heads
Daffodils
April showers bring May flowers
I wanted to write a springtime poem
giddy high school seniors
with six weeks to go
I wanted to write a poem about Love.

Love…Love…I wanted to write a poem about Love.

Nothing Can Break Me

I come from sweat, blood, tears
Zinc fence and Macca tree
I come from Holy Ghost filled, water baptized, Jesus on ma mind
I come from Dick Sea, Glenfinlas and Cross Roads
I come from Strong Back and Rice Bitters
I come from Sarsaparilla
Mint tea and Cerasee.

Nothing, Can Break Me.

I come from tuna shampoo
Coconut Oil greasing mi nappy head
I come from roast breadfruit
fried dumpling
chicken back and rice
I come from carrot juice an' lime
'cause there was no condensed milk.

Nothing, can break me
everything has been thrown at me
including the kitchen sink
take a good look at me
I am the queen of my own Universe
Jeremiah 29:11 is my favorite verse

what you see is what you get
You ain't see nothing yet.

Nothing, Can Break Me

Break me... break me...break me...

Nothing Can Break Me.

Tick...Tick...Tick...

Now the day is over
I crawl into bed
Tick… tick… tick… it's the only sound I hear
Body laced with joy, riddled with pain
Me
Downloading today's events
Inhaling the freshness of my own body
No talcum powers
Just the natural fragrance
Of my beautiful self
Often beaten down by the cares of the world
But, never taken out.

It's the daily reminders of racism, classism, sexism, trauma, bigotry
Absorbing the hurt and pain
My students super impose on my being
I don't mind, I really don't
they're young, they shouldn't be bogged down with stuff
like homelessness, low wages
Kids in cages
Only, they do
makes me mad. Sad.

I like to watch them in the hallways
We're in this together
Hurrying to class
Their joyful faces

The laughter, the giggles, the romping around … who cares about the second bell
Some do, others …well … not so much
They saunter with little worry that the classroom door will close in a minute
Their big contagious smiles as big as that Afro the boy is sporting
They've learned the art of smiling through their collective pain
Yes, the pain that is so intricately tied to the fleeting joys of our life.

Tick… tick… tick…
It's the only sound I hear
The old clock on the chest of drawers reminds me that time is fleeting
And, that my time on earth is finite
I hope I get to sleep tonight
Instead of tossing and turning thinking of the "what ifs"
As if "what ifs" can solve a darn thing.

I just ended a
Thirteen hour shift
But, who cares
My neighbor, just did a double
Making a measly $10:50 an hour
That's not even a living wage
Yet, she has no choice
She has a family to feed
God knows they live in constant need.

Tick…tick… tick…
It's the only sound I hear
It soothes my soul
While I unpack my fears
Silently hoping and praying my redemption is near
My life isn't as it appears
it's kind of like the sign on the rear view mirror
"Objects in mirror are closer than they appear."

So darn deceptive
"But it's life, Right?"

Hiding under the covers
Trying hard to recover from the pain of today's events
So much on my mind
Lots of stuff to rewind
I wish I could just turn off this bloody recorder of a mind
That's in constant rewind
Tick… tick… tick…
It's the only sound I hear
I just hope I get to sleep tonight.

Tonight… Tonight…Tonight…I just hope I get to sleep tonight.

Chapter Three

Who Is God?

Who is God?
What is God?
Where is God?
God of our fathers in distress.

"Is He the bird that flies so high?"
Or, is He a wandering child
Whose father doesn't care
If He lives or if He dies?"
"Is He a crystal ball or one that always fall?"

Now, stop your wondering
God is a God of love
Also of wrath
He's of the living
and not the dead.

He's the light of life
and, the resurrection
of all powers.
And, he that believeth on him
Should not perish
Because, He's the giver of life.

My first poem, and first place winner in our church's national competition (1974)

Searching

In the stillness of the morning
I find God
I find peace
I find myself
I find others
I find you.

Death

And, death comes crawling, crawling, gnawing, gnawing
Alone in the darkness of the night
But, can I stop it?
No, I can never stop it
So, quietly it comes and whispers
"Come, you must go with me."

"Come, you must go with me."
So, without another word
It held me by the hand
Into a land, that I had never seen
Heaven.

I wrote this poem immediately after dad passed away suddenly on October 27, 1982. It was less than a month after I entered St. Joseph's Teachers' College.

Wisdom

I know a very special man
Who could not read or write
Illiterate you could say
But, by no means uneducated
I know a very special man
He had more knowledge
Than most literate people I know
He was wise beyond his years
He was able to comprehend
The world in ways that was incomprehensible
I know a very special man
I call him, Dada.

Cecelia's

Over 30 and sexy
Smoke filled room
Grown people gyrating their bodies
Like teenagers
Trying to find their place in the universe
Non-alcoholic drinks
Unavailable
Juice-yes
Pineapple…juice
Maybe, maybe… not
Johnson, the African DJ spinning good "ole" Reggae music
Flies off the set
Just to wiggle his funny little self in those tight fitting pants
Reggae music, blasting, the Reggae beat pulsating to the rhythm of the soul
Dancing, laughter
Smoke filled room, young at heart
Over 30 and sexy.

Cecelia's was the night club in Providence that played the best Reggae Music in the early 90s.

Another World

To live
To Enjoy
To be a part of the universe
Another world
To help create
Equality
Fairness
Love for humanity
Reading maketh a man
That's what they say
How about a boy, a girl
A woman?
Maybe…maybe
One day we will create
Another world
Where everyone is equal.

Flip The Script

Who said that life
Was going to be easy
So many challenges
Money, love, no love, relationships
kids, no kids
Job, no job, want to find a job
Life, no life
Or, so it seems.
You shouldn't call all your friends over
for a pity party
misery loves company
anyway
Pray
that works
Most of the time
sometimes
all the time.
Today
Flip the script
Make it better
Take ownership of your life
Your destiny
What's the choice?
No choice
Flip the script.
Find God.

Happiness

Happiness is yours, if you can
Dream the big impossible dream
Twiddle your fingers, and not feel silly
Laugh at yourself
Dance to your own music
Play in the rain
Chase pretty painted butterflies
Sing praises to thy creator
Soar higher than the sky
Happiness is yours, if you can
Be yourself.

Suddenly

It suddenly dawned on me
That very soon
I won't have any more 15-17 pages IEP to write
No progress reports to sign
No more of those long meetings to sit in
No more mounds of papers covered my desk
No more forms to fill in
No more Medicaid billing
"Who am I?"
"A Paper Pusher?"
This is not what I signed up for
I want to be a Special Education Teacher
That's it
I want to engage in meaningful pedagogy
Connect with kids where they are
Lift them up
Infuse in them
Hope and Possibilities
Not buried in mountains of bureaucracy
There are days when I look at data
Wondering, what for, data aren't children.

It suddenly dawned on me
That I'm going to miss being a Special Education Teacher.

Me Too

I believe you
You're my mother, sister, aunt, friend
Woman
I believed you when
You say he'd harassed you, assaulted you.
You're a survivor, not a victim
And, what if you can't remember the minute, the hour, the day
Does it make your story less truthful, less credible?
No, you do not have to remember the minute, the hour, the day
Heck, you don't have to remember what you wore
That has no relevance to your credibility
I believe you.

You tried and failed to rob her of her virginity
Her dignity
I cringe at the humiliation she endures
While culprits like you get undue adoration
Some women will never, share their story
Will never open up about the violence or assault they confront every day
It's high time we believe women.
Believe Women…Believe Women…Believe… Women.

The Poems I Lost

I mourn for the poems I have lost…
I hope they are somewhere, in the atmosphere
Being told to little boys and girls
To teach them about living
Teach them about God
Teach them that all of their dreams can go far.

To all my lost poems…
I hope you roam and roam
Until you find a home in the atmosphere
Teach kids to have no fear
Their dreams will go far…

By. Terrence Vassell

I was telling my son that I mourn for the poems that I lost. He penned this poem dedicated to the poems that I lost.

A Mother's Heart

A mother's heart is loving and kind
A rare gem, one of a kind
A mother's heart loves to the bitter end
A mother's heart will always be your friend.

A mother's heart is resilient
Not easily bent
See that mother
Oh brother!
She wakes up and hustles every single day
Making a measly
$10.50 an hour for her pay
She never complains
She knows her struggle ain't in vain.

Watch her stride
So much grace, so much pride
You can't control her
She's in control of her own universe
She wraps herself in love
She has protection from above.

Old mother, middle aged mother, young mother
Earth mother
We're all indebted to you
Your womb protects us from the storms of life
Making sure we stay safe amidst the strife.

Our lives have been complicated
Fabricated
Often Miss- understood
No one has been able to overstand the complexity of womanhood
It's how we survive
Confusing the enemy
It's called Mama Mode
Standing watch over our brood.

Thank you, Woman
Rich...Woman
Poor...Woman
White...Woman
Black...Woman
Transgender... Woman
Woman stepping up and stepping out -filling the gap, of
That woman that life has done a number on
It ain't because she did nothing wrong
It's because the decks have been stacked up against her
Because she's... Woman
Pushing against the wind of patriarchy, misogyny
Resisting a system that has never protected her or her kind
A system that to her has been grossly... unkind.

There's no retreat for us
None of us
We've got each other
When our back's jammed up against the wall
When all we can do is holla and bawl
Don't take our tears for weakness
These are the tears of a woman's heart
Making a comeback right from the start
You, yes you who have tried to bully us
To render us silent, invisible
We're not weak
Don't misconstrue

Our tears as such
Our strength…as solid as a rock
The rock of Gibraltar
We will never be defeated
We're women indomitable.

A mother's heart
Filled with love
A mother's heart filled with pain
Crying for the children she's lost
To senseless, totally preventable - gun violence
A mother's heart waiting to be touched, caressed
A mother's heart waiting to be loved
A mother's heart so gentle, so bold
A mother's heart
If only the world could fully believe, trust, appreciate and understand …
A Mother's Heart.

Mothers' Day
May 12, 2019
6:55 AM

Glossary

Walker's Wood Jerk Sauce: A hot spicy Jamaican sauce made from herbs and spices and can be used for flavoring in meats, soups or vegetarian meals

Gungo peas- Pigeon Peas

Mi- I

Yuh- You

Oxtail- The cow's tail, a favorite Jamaican meat, mostly served with white rice or rice and peas for lunch or dinner

Macca- thorns

Ma- My

Dick Sea- The name of the beach not too far from where I lived, I would walk to the beach to romp in the sand or splash in the water

Glenfinlas- An open acre or more of empty space that had mangoes, ackees, sweetsop and other fruit trees. As kids we would walk to Glenfinlas to get fruits, the scariest part of going to pick mangoes would be having to pass the green lizards

Cross Road- The neighborhood square where people would congregate mostly to socialize or to catch the bus to Town (Kingston)

Strong Back – tuber that grows in the ground and has medicinal values. One year when I was too sick to go to school, I accompanied my grandmother to "root up" Strong Back so she could sell at the market. Strong Back can be used for making tea

Cerassee- Green herb used to make tea, excellent for belly aches or menstrual cramps

Rice Bitters: Herb used to make tea, has bitterish taste, good for colds or congestive illnesses

Sarsaparilla- herb used to make tea

Breadfruit – not really a fruit -originated in West Africa, can be cooked or roasted usually over wood fire, often served for breakfast with Ackee and Saltfish but can be boiled as well in soups

Ackee- Jamaica's national dish, compared to scrambled eggs

Dumplings- made from flour, mixed with baking powder for frying, can also be cooked, minus the baking powder

Nanny of the Maroons- (c. 1686-1755) Jamaica's only female national Shero. Nanny was an 18th century Asante (present day Ghana)Warrior

Cotton Gins- A machine used for separating cotton from the seeds, an instrument for the enslaved people who worked for free on the plantations

Ashanti : An ethnic group

Asanteewaa- An Asante Warrior

Lillian Mignott- My maternal grandmother, she had seven children

Ellen Euphema Spencer- my paternal grandmother, she had ten children

Mavis the Ranglin Warrior- My mom

Dada- Dad

Peas Soup- Soup that can be made with broad beans, red peas (beans) or gungo peas (pigeon peas). Pig tail or salted beef can be added for extra flavor. Peas soup can be strictly vegetarian as well

Porridge- cooked cereal made with oat meal, corn meal or green bananas or oats

Carrot Juice- grated and then juiced, sweetened with condensed milk, line can be used instead of condensed milk for a light refreshing drink

Potato Pudding- a dessert, served for breakfast or lunch, mom would bake potato pudding and she would give it to us to take to school for lunch (I hated taking it to school as it was a sure way of telling you had no money to pay for lunches, but it was so good)

Rice and Peas and chicken – A favorite Jamaican Sunday dinner

Callaloo- a vegetable much like spinach, steamed over low flame, can be served for breakfast, lunch or dinner, can also be used to make pepper pot soup

Button Bay- Dad had acres of land which he cultivated with fruits and vegetables, it's where he also raised his livestock such as cows, goats and horses. As kids we would dread walking to Button Bay but had no choice but to help dad in the field around crop time.

Lignum Vitae- indigenous to the Caribbean and it's the Jamaican national flower.

Rock of Gibraltar- symbol of strength

Chicken Back- For many poor families, chicken back was the only meat they had frequently, it was inexpensive but so good when it was curried with scotch bonnet pepper, and all the other rich authentic seasoning